**DISCOVERY EDUCATION** | SCIENCE TECHBOOK

# California
# Unit 1
Landscape Shapes

To obtain permission(s) or for inquiries, submit a request to:
Discovery Education, Inc.
4350 Congress Street, Suite 700
Charlotte, NC  28209
800-323-9084
Education_Info@DiscoveryEd.com

ISBN 13: 978-1-68220-537-2

Printed in the United States of America.

 3 4 5 6 7 8 9 10  CWM  27 26 25 24 23 22     B

**Acknowledgments**

Acknowledgment is given to photographers, artists, and agents for permission to feature their copyrighted material.

Cover and inside cover art: Galyna Andrushko / Shutterstock.com

© Discovery Education | www.discoveryeducation.com

# Table of Contents

# Dear Parent/Guardian,

This year, your student will be using Science Techbook™, a comprehensive science program developed by the educators and designers at Discovery Education and written to the California Next Generation Science Standards (NGSS). The California NGSS expect students to act and think like scientists and engineers, to ask questions about the world around them, and to solve real-world problems through the application of critical thinking across the domains of science (Life Science, Earth and Space Science, Physical Science).

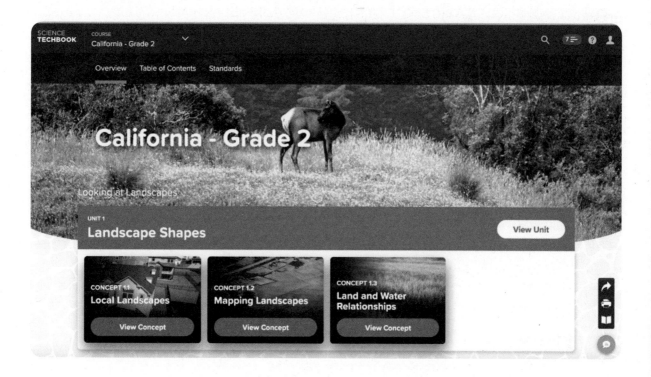

Science Techbook is an innovative program that helps your student master key scientific concepts. Students engage with interactive science materials to analyze and interpret data, think critically, solve problems, and make connections across science disciplines. Science Techbook includes dynamic content, videos, digital tools, Hands-On Activities and labs, and gamelike activities that inspire and motivate scientific learning and curiosity.

You and your child can access the resource by signing in to www.discoveryeducation.com. You can view your child's progress in the course by selecting the Assignment button.

Science Techbook is divided into units, and each unit is divided into concepts. Each concept has three sections: Wonder, Learn, and Share.

**Units and Concepts** Students begin to consider the connections across fields of science to understand, analyze, and describe real-world phenomena.

**Wonder** Students activate their prior knowledge of a concept's essential ideas and begin making connections to a real-world phenomenon and the **Can You Explain?** question.

**Learn** Students dive deeper into how real-world science phenomenon works through critical reading of the Core Interactive Text. Students also build their learning through Hands-On Activities and interactives focused on the learning goals.

**Share** Students share their learning with their teacher and classmates using evidence they have gathered and analyzed during Learn. Students connect their learning with STEM careers and problem-solving skills.

**Discovery**
EDUCATION

Within this Student Edition, you'll find QR codes and quick codes that take you and your student to a corresponding section of Science Techbook online. To use the QR codes, you'll need to download a free QR reader. Readers are available for phones, tablets, laptops, desktops, and other devices. Most use the device's camera, but there are some that scan documents that are on your screen.

For resources in California Science Techbook, you'll need to sign in with your student's username and password the first time you access a QR code. After that, you won't need to sign in again, unless you log out or remain inactive for too long.

We encourage you to support your student in using the print and online interactive materials in Science Techbook on any device. Together, may you and your student enjoy a fantastic year of science!

Sincerely,

**The Discovery Education Science Team**

# Unit 1
# Landscape Shapes

# Storm Water Capture

Did you know that a snow-covered mountain can affect the amount of water people have who live many miles away? In this unit, you will look at how land and water are related. At the end of the unit, you will be able to use this information to design a storm water capture system as a solution for areas that have too much drought.

**Watch** the video about why snowfall in winter is important to stopping drought in the summer.

Quick Code: ca2006s

Video

Storm Water Capture

**Discovery** EDUCATION

## Think About It

**Look** at the photograph. **Think** about the following question:

- How can we describe the shape of land and water on Earth?

Lake in the Mountains

## Design Solutions Like a Scientist

Quick Code:
ca2005s

### Hands-On Engineering:
### Capturing Runoff from Landscapes

In this activity, you will design a way to collect storm water runoff. You will then tell how the captured runoff can help a place that has drought.

Water Runoff

| SEP | Developing and Using Models | CCC | Systems and System Models |
| SEP | Constructing Explanations and Designing Solutions | CCC | Patterns |

## Ask Questions About the Problem

You are going to design a solution to capture and save water so it can be used in a drought. **Write** some questions you can ask to learn more about the problem. As you work on activities throughout the unit, **write** down answers to your questions.

# Local
# Landscapes

## Student Objectives

By the end of this lesson:

- [ ] I can study land elevations to see how their size relates to slope.

- [ ] I can use what I see and learn to compare the sizes of landforms to the sizes of bodies of water.

- [ ] I can make a model to show different landforms.

- [ ] I can use math to compare shapes in different landforms.

## Key Vocabulary

- [ ] canyon
- [ ] characteristic
- [ ] elevation
- [ ] feature
- [ ] landform
- [ ] landscape
- [ ] mountain

- [ ] naturalist
- [ ] ocean
- [ ] plain
- [ ] plateau
- [ ] preserve
- [ ] quadrilateral
- [ ] river

- [ ] slope
- [ ] stream
- [ ] valley

Quick Code:
ca2007s

### Activity 1
## Can You Explain?

How are landforms and bodies of water alike and different?

_____

_____

_____

_____

_____

Quick Code:
ca2009s

DISCOVERY
EDUCATION

**Activity 2**

# Ask Questions Like a Scientist

Quick Code:
ca2010s

## Landscapes

**Look** at the photo. **Answer** the questions.

Let's Investigate Landscapes

© Discovery Education | www.discoveryeducation.com • Image: IP Galantemik D.U / E+ / Getty Images; National Archives

| SEP | Planning and Carrying Out Investigations |
| SEP | Asking Questions and Defining Problems |

EDUCATION

Artists who take photos think about the shapes of objects. What lines and shapes do you see?

_____

_____

**Trace** the shapes in the photo with a pencil. What else can you say about them?

_____

_____

What questions do you have about the place and landforms in the photo?

> **Your Questions**
>
>
>
>
>
>
>
>
>

# Make Shapes

You can draw on a photo to see different shapes in the land. Just like a picture, the land around us has many different shapes. The overall shape of the land is called a **landscape**.

Landscapes come in many different shapes. The big shapes you see on Earth often change slowly over time. But you can make small changes with your own hands in your garden or yard.

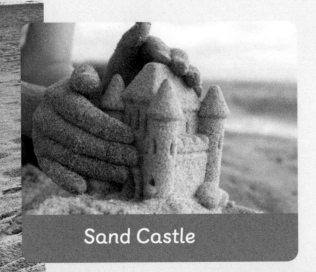

Sand Castle

Many people like to shape the earth at the beach too. They use their hands and other tools to shape sand into different forms.

| **Discovery** EDUCATION

## Activity 3
# Analyze Like a Scientist

Quick Code:
ca2011s

## Make Shapes

**Think** about what you have read and the pictures you have seen.

What forms could you make with sand?

_____

_____

**Draw** your ideas for some forms you can make with sand.

```
┌─────────────────────────────────────────────┐
│                                               │
│                                               │
│                                               │
│                                               │
│                                               │
│                                               │
│                                               │
│                                               │
└─────────────────────────────────────────────┘
```

**SEP**   Constructing Explanations and Designing Solutions

**CCC**   Stability and Change

### Activity 4
# Think Like a Scientist

Quick Code:
ca2012s

## Digging in the Sand

In this activity, you will model different shapes of **landforms** by molding a mixture of sand and water with your hands. You will develop an understanding of how landforms look like many shapes.

### What materials do you need? (per group)
- Sand
- Water
- Aluminum foil pan, 13×9×2
- Plastic cup, 9 oz
- Camera
- Plastic sandwich bag

**Write** a goal of this activity.

_____

_____

_____

| SEP | Planning and Carrying Out Investigations | CCC | Patterns |
| --- | --- | --- | --- |

## What Will You Do?

**Look** at the pictures of landforms.

**Trace** three different shapes you will model with sand.

Shapes of Landforms

**Fill** the pan with sand.

**Add** a cup of water to the sand.

**Mix** the sand and water.

**Model** your three different landforms.

**Draw** pictures of your models.

| | |
|---|---|
| Model 1 | |
| Model 2 | |
| Model 3 | |

**Think About It**

**Compare** your landscape models.

How were your landscapes the same?

_____

_____

_____

_____

How were your landscapes different?

_____

_____

_____

_____

What patterns did you see?

_____

_____

_____

_____

### Activity 5
# Observe Like a Scientist

Quick Code:
ca2013s

## Largest Sand Castle

**Watch** the video. **Look** for shapes in the sand castle.

Largest Sand Castle

## Talk Together

Now, talk together about the shapes you saw. What shapes did you see the most?

Quick Code:
ca2014s

### Activity 6
# Observe Like a Scientist

## Rocks in the Landscape

**Look** at the picture of this landscape.
**Point** to some different forms you can see.

Rocks in the Landscape

What does the landscape look like where you live?

### Activity 7
# Evaluate Like a Scientist

Quick Code:
ca2015s

## What Do You Already Know About Local Landscapes?

### Discussing Water and Land

**Think** about places you have been. What types of land have you seen?

_____

_____

_____

### Where do you find water?

_____

_____

_____

# What Shape Is It?

**Look** at the pictures. **Classify** each by shape. **Write** *circle, triangle,* or *quadrilateral* below each picture.

_____

_____

_____

_____

_____

_____

# Slope in a Landscape

Suppose you want to have a picnic lunch in the schoolyard. To be comfortable, you want to spread your blanket on level ground. Think about your schoolyard. There may be places where the ground slopes. There may be other places where the ground is flat. A flat place would be best for a picnic.

Landforms are the physical **features** on Earth's surface. In some places, the land **slopes**. You may find that water collects at the bottom of a slope. This is because water flows toward lower ground. In other places, the land is flat.

Coastline

**Elevation** is the height of a landform above or below sea level. Landforms are described by their shape and elevation.

# How Can We Find Slope in Landscapes?

---

**Activity 8**
## Analyze Like a Scientist

Quick Code: ca2017s

## Slope in a Landscape

**Look** around your schoolyard. Where have you seen water collect in puddles?

_____

_____

_____

What do you think this tells you about the landscape?

_____

_____

_____

**Activity 9**
# Investigate Like a Scientist

Quick Code:
ca2018s

## Hands-On Investigation: Finding Slopes

In this activity, you will explore different areas of elevation outside. You will develop an understanding of how scale and proportion relate to slope.

**Make a Prediction**

You are going to observe places with high and low elevation around you. **Write** or **draw** your predictions.

Where do you predict you will see low or flat elevations?

Where do you predict you will see high elevations?

**What materials do you need?** (per group)

- Tennis balls
- Water
- Plastic cup, 9 oz

## What Will You Do?

**Look** for an area to test in your schoolyard. **Use** the ball to test the elevation. What happened?

_____

_____

_____

Now **use** the water to test the elevation. What happened?

_____

_____

_____

**SEP** Planning and Carrying Out Investigations

**CCC** Patterns

**CCC** Scale, Proportion, and Quantity

How did you find the high and low areas of elevation?
**Write** or **draw** how you found the high and low places of elevation.

| High Elevation |
| --- |
|  |

| Low Elevation |
| --- |
|  |

**Discovery** EDUCATION

## Think About the Activity

How were areas of high and low elevation the same?
How were areas of high and low elevation different?

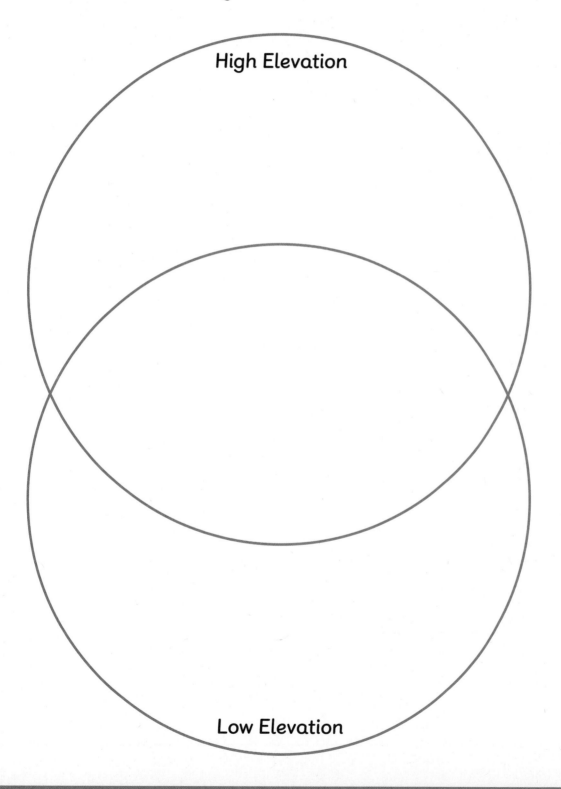

High Elevation

Low Elevation

What patterns did you see?

_____

_____

_____

**Draw** a place in your schoolyard that has both a high and low elevation.

**Discovery**
EDUCATION

# How Can We Look Closer at Different Land and Water Forms?

### Activity 10
## Observe Like a Scientist

Quick Code: ca2019s

## Landforms: Introduction

**Watch** the video. **Look** for different types of landforms.

Video

Landforms: Introduction

 **Talk Together**

Now, talk together about the different landforms you have seen where you live. What do they look like?

© Discovery Education | www.discoveryeducation.com • Image: IP Galanternik D.U / E+ / Getty Images, Pixabay, Icon: Freepik from www.flaticon.com

**Activity 11**
# Think Like a Scientist

Quick Code:
ca2020s

## Landscape Board

In this activity, you will find information about landforms and water forms. You will show how these landforms are organized from small to large. You will make a board to share your landforms with the class.

### What materials do you need? (per group)

- Pencils
- Access to the Internet
- Optional print resources of landforms and water features

## What Will You Do?

**Find** information about four different landforms and four different water forms. Where will you look?

_____

_____

**Record** the information you find in your science journals.

CCC   Scale, Proportion, and Quantity

© Discovery Education | www.discoveryeducation.com · Image: IP Galanternik D.U / E+ / Getty Images

**Put** the landforms in order from lowest to highest elevation.

**Draw** and **write** about each landform.

| Landform Drawing | About the Landform |
| --- | --- |
|  |  |
|  |  |
|  |  |
|  |  |

**Put** the water forms in order from smallest to largest.

**Draw** and **write** about each water form.

| Water Form Drawing | About the Water Form |
|---|---|
|  |  |
|  |  |
|  |  |
|  |  |

**Make** a board to show what you found out about landforms and water forms. How did you build the board? **Tell** or **draw** the steps you took.

## Think About the Activity

**Share** your work with the class. How are your water forms and landforms the same?

_____

_____

_____

How are your water forms and landforms different?

_____

_____

_____

What patterns did you see?

_____

_____

_____

## Activity 12
# Observe Like a Scientist

Quick Code: ca2021s

## Plains and Plateaus

**Watch** the video. **Look** for how the sizes and shapes of the different landforms are related.

Video

Plains and Plateaus

### Talk Together

Now, talk together about the plains and plateaus you saw. How are they the same or different?

### Activity 13
# Observe Like a Scientist

Quick Code:
ca2022s

## Earth's Water Features

**Watch** the video. **Look** at the sizes and shapes of the different water forms.

Video

Earth's Water Features

 **Talk Together**

Now, talk together about the different water forms you saw. How do Earth's water features compare in size?

### Activity 14
# Observe Like a Scientist

Quick Code:
ca2023s

## Valleys and Canyons

**Watch** the video. **Look** for how the sizes and shapes of the different landforms are related.

Video

**Valleys and Canyons**

 **Talk Together**

Now, talk together about the valleys and canyons you saw. How are they the same or different?

# Comparing Land and Water Forms

There are many different types of landforms. You can compare them.

- **Plains** are large, wide, flat areas. A **plateau** is wide and flat like a plain, but it has a higher elevation.

- A **mountain** is a landform with a narrow top and steep sides that is much higher than the land around it. A hill is like a mountain, but it is much shorter.

- **Valleys** and canyons are lowlands between hills or mountains. The difference between them is that valleys have a gentle slope, while **canyons** are deep and narrow.

- Water features include **streams**, **rivers**, and **oceans**. A river is larger than a stream. An ocean is larger than a river.

Think about how these compare with the local landforms and water features near you.

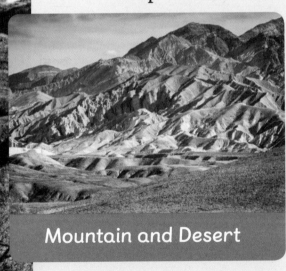

**Mountain and Desert**

## Activity 15
## Analyze Like a Scientist

Quick Code:
ca2024s

## Comparing Land and Water Forms

**Think** about what you have read and the pictures you have seen. If you were to take a trip, which landforms or water features would you like to visit? Why?

_____

_____

_____

**Draw** yourself doing something in the place you would like to visit.

### Activity 16
# Evaluate Like a Scientist

Quick Code:
ca2025s

## Rivers, Lakes, and Marshes

**Look** at the pictures. **Classify** each water form. **Write** *river*, *lake*, or *marsh* below each picture.

_____

_____

_____

_____

© Discovery Education | www.discoveryeducation.com • Image: IP Galanternik D.U / E+ / Getty Images, Paul Fuqua, David R.White / Shutterstock.com, Edelwipix / Shutterstock.com, Sundry Photography / Shutterstock.com

**CCC**   Patterns

**Choose** one of the pictures. **Write** a caption for the image. Your caption should make someone want to visit the location shown.

_____

_____

_____

_____

# Making Models of Landscapes

A model is a tool that can be used to explain how different objects interact. A girl pouring water into a bowl can be a model of how water flows from rivers to lakes. The water travels through the spout of the pitcher downward into the bowl.

River water travels downhill. It empties into low, level areas called basins. When water collects in the basin, it forms a lake. Rivers can carry water into and out of lakes. Think about how the shapes of the objects in the model are like the shapes of a river and a lake.

Pouring Water

# How Can We Use Shapes to Show How Landforms Work?

**Activity 17**
## Analyze Like a Scientist

Quick Code:
ca2026s

## Making Models of Landscapes

**Look** at the picture of the girl making her model. What part of the model represents the river? What part represents the lake?

How can you make this model better?

### Activity 18
# Investigate Like a Scientist

Quick Code:
ca2027s

## Hands-On Investigation: Making a River and a Lake

In this activity, you will make a model of a river and a lake. You will use them to tell how the bodies of water are alike or different.

**Make a Prediction**

**Write** or **draw** your predictions.

What materials will work best for your models?

What shapes will you need?

| SEP | Developing and Using Models | | CCC | Systems and System Models |
|-----|-----------------------------|--|-----|---------------------------|

**What materials do you need?** (per group)

- Modeling clay
- Aluminum foil pan, 13×9×2
- Pitcher
- Water

## What Will You Do?

**Draw** a plan for your model of a lake.
**Use** clay to build the model.

<br>

**Use** the pitcher of water to fill the lake. What happened?

_____

_____

_____

**Draw** a plan for your model of a river. **Use** clay to build the model.

**Use** the pitcher of water to make the river flow. What happened?

_____

_____

_____

## Think About the Activity

How are rivers and lakes the same?
How are rivers and lakes different?

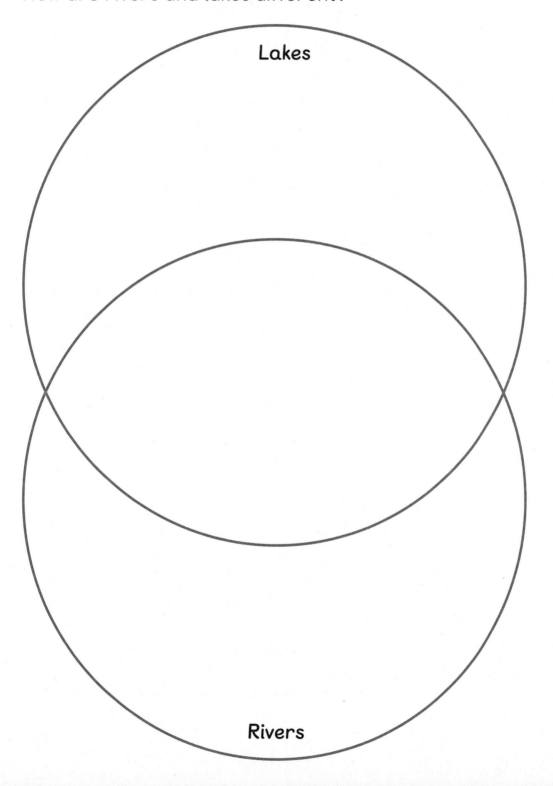

Lakes

Rivers

How did your model show the ways bodies of water are alike or different?

_____

_____

_____

_____

_____

**Discovery** EDUCATION

Draw a model to describe how elevation can change the flow of water.

### Activity 19
# Observe Like a Scientist

Quick Code:
ca2028s

## Stone Wall

**Look** at the picture of this wall made of stones. What shapes do you see?

Stone Wall

**Draw** some of the different shapes you can see in the wall.
**Label** the shapes.

Landforms can be made of more than one shape. What shapes can make up a mountain?

**Activity 20**
## Observe Like a Scientist

Quick Code:
ca2029s

## Mesa

**Look** at the picture of a mesa.

Mesa

What shape do you see? **Draw** the shape.

© Discovery Education | www.discoveryeducation.com • Image: IP Galanternik D.U / E+ / Getty Images; Paul Fuqua

## Activity 21
# Evaluate Like a Scientist

Quick Code:
ca2030s

## Landform Shapes

**Look** at the pictures. **Classify** each by shape. **Write**
*circle*, *triangle*, or *quadrilateral* below each picture.
Some can be more than one shape.

_____

_____

_____

_____

_____

_____

_____

_____

_____

_____

**SEP** Developing and Using Models

### Activity 22
# Record Evidence Like a Scientist

Quick Code:
ca2031s

## Landscapes

Now that you have learned about landforms and bodies of water, **look** again at the Let's Investigate Landscapes photo.

Let's Investigate Landscapes

### Talk Together

How can you describe landscapes now? How is your explanation different from before?

**SEP** **Constructing Explanations and Designing Solutions**

**Look** at the Can You Explain? question. You first read this question at the beginning of the lesson.

>
>
> ## Can You Explain?
>
> How are landforms and bodies of water alike and different?

Now, you will **use** your new ideas about Let's Investigate Landscapes to answer a question.

1. **Choose** a question. You can use the Can You Explain? question, or one of your own. You can also use one of the questions that you wrote at the beginning of the lesson.

**Your Question**

2. Then, **use** the sentence starters on the next page to answer the question.

Mountains, hills, plateaus, plains, valleys, and canyons

_____

_____

_____

Some landforms

_____

_____

_____

while others

_____

_____

_____

I can compare landforms

_____

_____

_____

Rivers, streams, lakes, and oceans

_____

_____

_____

Some bodies of water

_____

_____

_____

while others

_____

_____

_____

The evidence I collected

_____

_____

_____

 **in Action**

**Activity 23**

# Analyze Like a Scientist

## Ansel Adams: Naturalist and Photographer

**Read** the story. Which sentence tells how Ansel Adams helps us want to protect nature? **Circle** the sentence.

 **Read Together**

# Ansel Adams: Naturalist and Photographer

Ansel Adams was born in California in 1902. He took photos of nature for a living. He is most known for the many black and white landscape photos he took of the American West. Adams took photos of landforms in places such as Yosemite National Park and Glacier National Park. By focusing on light and shape, Adams' photos showed the beauty of nature. Adams died in 1984. His photos help people see why we should protect our beautiful environment.

**Peak Above Woody Lake, Kings River Canyon**

**Look** at the photo by Ansel Adams.

Peak Above Woody Lake,
Kings River Canyon

How do people who take photos of nature help us learn about landforms and water forms?

_____

_____

_____

Why do their photos help us want to protect nature?

_____

_____

_____

## All About the Details

Thalia sees this photo in a nature book. She shows it to her friend and points out the land and water forms.

Kings River Canyon

**Look** at the sentences below. Which ones could Thalia have said to her friend?

**Check** all that apply.

☐ There are many hills in this landscape.

☐ At the bottom of the mountain there is a plateau.

☐ I can see canyons are in this landscape.

☐ The mountains look like triangles.

☐ A river runs through the mountains.

☐ Trees and plants are growing on the mountainside.

How did you decide which sentences were correct?

_____

_____

_____

**Activity 24**
# Evaluate Like a Scientist

Quick Code:
ca2036s

## Review: Local Landscapes

**Think** about what you have read and seen. What did you learn?

**Draw** what you have learned. Then, **tell** someone else about what you learned.

 **Talk Together**

Think about what you saw in Get Started. Use your new ideas to discuss local landscapes.

**CCC** **Patterns**

# Mapping Landscapes

## Student Objectives

By the end of this lesson:

☐ I can study maps to find out how they show patterns in real-world objects.

☐ I can make two-dimensional maps that model three-dimensional landforms and water features.

☐ I can make an argument, using evidence, to say why a map is a good model of a real-world object.

## Key Vocabulary

☐ location

☐ map

☐ model

☐ relief map

☐ two-dimensional

Quick Code:
ca2037s

## Activity 1
## Can You Explain?

How can you show the location of landforms and water features?

_____

_____

_____

_____

_____

Quick Code:
ca2039s

### Activity 2
## Ask Questions Like a Scientist

Quick Code:
ca2040s

## Landscapes in Animation

**Look** at the photo. **Answer** the questions.

Let's Investigate Landscapes in Animation

© Discovery Education | www.discoveryeducation.com • Image: Kazakova_Helga / Shutterstock.com, Photography by Mangiwau / Moment Open / Getty Images

 **SEP**  Asking Questions and Defining Problems

What objects in the picture give you clues to what happens in the story?

_____

_____

_____

_____

What questions do you have about landscapes in animation?

**Your Questions**

© Discovery Education | www.discoveryeducation.com • Image: Photography by Mangiwau / Moment Open / Getty Images

**Activity 3**
# Think Like a Scientist

Quick Code:
ca2041s

## Landscape of a Setting

In this activity, you will make a landscape based on a setting found in a book you have read.

**What materials do you need?** (per group)

- Shoebox lid or tray
- Modeling clay
- Paper
- Pencils
- Crayons

**SEP**   Developing and Using Models

## What Will You Do?

**Think** about the setting in your book. What materials can you use to add details to your landscape?

**Make** a list.

_____

_____

_____

_____

_____

**Draw** a landscape scene from the book that shows the setting. Use the clay to **build** your landscape setting in the shoebox lid.

**Read** the story to check that your setting is complete. Add any details you may have missed.

**Write** about your landscape setting.
What landforms did you build?

_____

_____

_____

Where are the landforms located?

_____

_____

_____

When you make a model it does not look exactly like the real-world object you are trying to show.

Now that you have built your model, **record** your landscape model on paper.

## Think About the Activity

Why are landscape and setting important when telling a story in a movie? **Write** or **draw** in the bubble chart to answer the question.

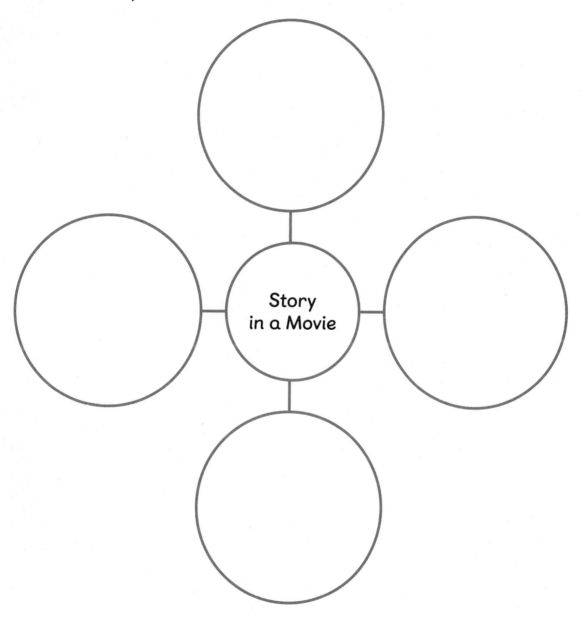

Story
in a Movie

Quick Code:
ca2042s

## Landscape in Movies

**Read** about landscapes in animations. Then, **answer** the question that follows.

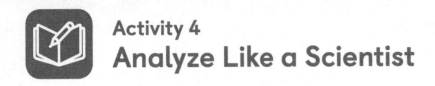

Read Together

# Landscape in Movies

Making things with clay or modeling dough can be a lot of fun. You can make a bowl, a pot, or maybe an animal. You could even make a movie using clay animation.

**SEP**  Obtaining, Evaluating, and Communicating Information

**CCC**  Scale, Proportion, and Quantity

© Discovery Education | www.discoveryeducation.com • Image: wararat_photos / Shutterstock.com. Icon: Freepik from www.flaticon.com

To do this, you would need to think of a good story. Think about where the story happens. This is the setting of the story. The characters in the story could move around in the landscape you create.

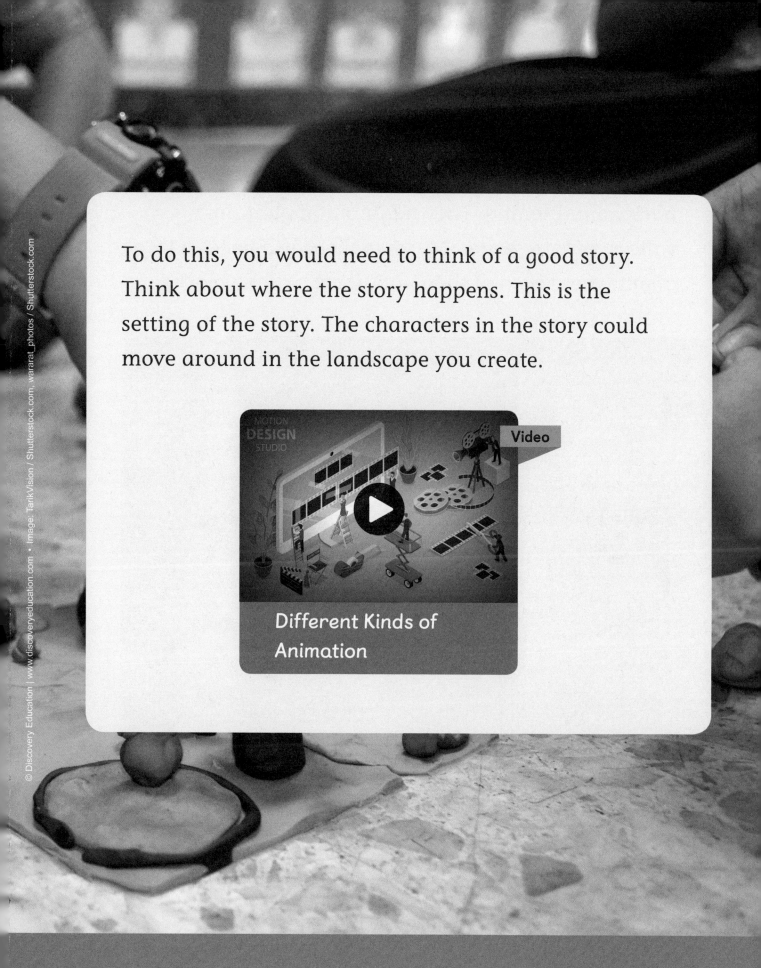

Video

Different Kinds of Animation

**Read Together**

Movie makers decide what landforms to put in the background setting. They might put mountains, valleys, hills, or water. Movie makers also need to think about where each of these landforms will be placed.

Lake Tahoe

If you made a movie using clay animation, what would the landscape look like? You could share your ideas with others using drawings. **Draw** or **write** your ideas.

### Activity 5
## Evaluate Like a Scientist

Quick Code:
ca2043s

## What Do You Already Know About Mapping Landscapes?

### How Are Land and Water Different?

Earth has water and land.

**Look** at the pictures. **Write** *water* or *land* below each picture.

_____

_____

_____

_____

_____

_____

_____

_____

_____

_____

**Mapping It Out**

What is a model?

_____

_____

_____

_____

How is a map a model?

_____

_____

_____

_____

How can maps be used to help us understand the world around us?

_____

_____

_____

_____

# How Do Maps Show Objects in the Real World?

### Activity 6
## Observe Like a Scientist

Quick Code:
ca2045s

## California Coastline

**Look** at the landscape in the photo. **Circle** a land or water feature you know. **Say** what is it called.

Northern California Coastline at Crescent City

| SEP | Analyzing and Interpreting Data | CCC | Patterns |

How is this landscape the same or different from the landscape where you live?

**Write** or **draw** in the table to answer the question.

| Same | | |
|------|------|------|
| Shape | Color | Object |
| | | |
| **Different** | | |
| Shape | Color | Object |
| | | |

## Activity 7
# Observe Like a Scientist

Quick Code:
ca2046s

## Different Kinds of Maps

**Watch** the video about **maps**. A map is a model of a place on Earth. **Look** for different information that maps can show.

Video

Different Kinds of Maps

### Talk Together

Now, talk together about the different kinds of maps you've seen. What kind of map have you used? Why did you use it?

**SEP**   Engaging in Argument from Evidence

**Read** each of the claims. There are three claims that are true and one that is false.

From the evidence you observed, **select** the claim that is false.

- Maps that show the boundaries of countries and states are called political maps.

- People who fly airplanes in the sky use maps.

- A service map will not help you determine the climate of an area.

- For a map to be useful, it should be two-dimensional or flat.

### Activity 8
# Think Like a Scientist

Quick Code:
ca2047s

## Compare Maps

In this activity, you will compare maps and look for patterns.

**What materials do you need?** (per group)
- Two or more basic maps
- Sticky notes
- Pencils

## What Will You Do?

**Look** at a map. A map is a flat, or **two-dimensional**, model of a place on Earth. What things can you see on a map?

SEP   Developing and Using Models

CCC   Patterns

CCC   Scale, Proportion, and Quantity

© Discovery Education | www.discoveryeducation.com • Image: Photography by Mangiwau / Moment Open / Getty Images

**Look** at the key or legend on a map. **Circle** some things you can find using the key.

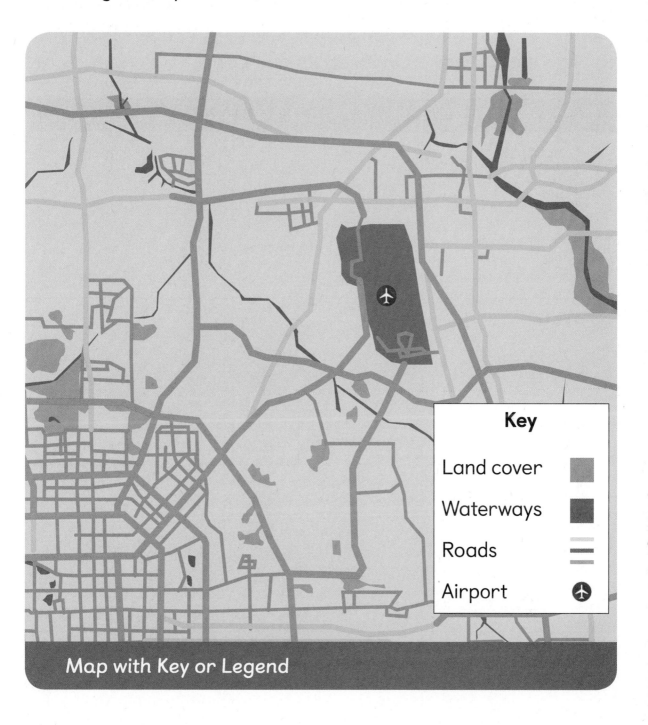

**Map with Key or Legend**

Key

Land cover

Waterways

Roads

Airport ✈

## Think About the Activity

**Look** at two different maps. **Think** about the **location** of different features. The location of the features helps you know where you can find them. **Draw** or **write** about each map.

| Observations | Map 1 | Map 2 |
|---|---|---|
| Location | | |
| Water | | |
| Land | | |
| Other Features | | |

DISCOVERY
EDUCATION

# How Are Maps Used to Show Landscapes?

 **Activity 9**
## Observe Like a Scientist

Quick Code: ca2048s

### Making a Raised Relief Map

**Watch** the video about relief maps. A relief map is a three-dimensional map. **Look** for strategies the students used to make their maps.

Making a Raised Relief Map

 **Talk Together**

Now, talk together about different areas on the map. How do the students decide where to place the clay and symbols?

**CCC** Scale, Proportion, and Quantity

### Activity 10
## Observe Like a Scientist

Quick Code:
ca2049s

## Model Train Landscape

**Look** at the picture of this model train landscape. It shows both hills and flat land.

**Circle** a hill. **Draw a square** around some flat land.

Model Train Landscape (Bird's Eye View)

© Discovery Education | www.discoveryeducation.com • Image: Rafael Elias / Moment Open / Getty Images, Photography by Mangiwau / Moment Open / Getty Images

SEP   Using Mathematics and Computational Thinking

CCC   Scale, Proportion, and Quantity

**Use** the lines to help you **compare** the hills and flat land on the picture of the model.

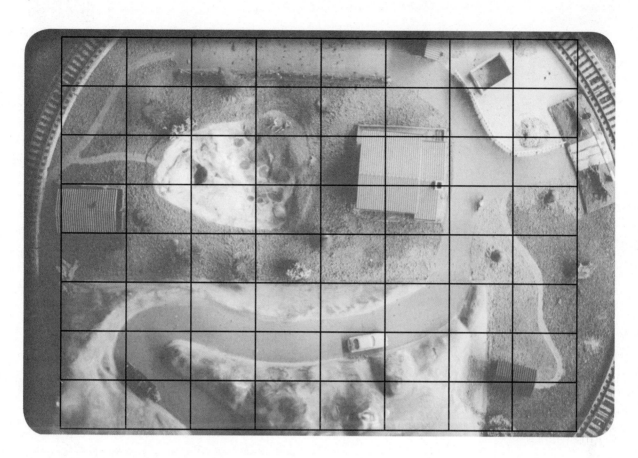

Are there more hills or flat land?

_____

How do you know?

_____

_____

_____

**Activity 11**
# Think Like a Scientist

Quick Code:
ca2050s

## A Landscape Map

In this activity, you will make a map of a landscape. Then you will use a map to build a different landscape.

**What materials do you need?** (per group)

- Shoebox lid or tray
- Modeling clay
- Paper
- Pencils
- Crayons
- Camera

You are going to make a map of a landscape. **Write** or **draw** your plan.

SEP   Developing and Using Models

**What Will You Do?**

**Design** a landscape.

**Use** different colors of clay to build a model of the landscape.

What features will you include? **Check** all the features you will use.

- ☐ Mountain
- ☐ River
- ☐ Valley
- ☐ Lake
- ☐ Road
- ☐ Forest

- ☐ Stream
- ☐ Ocean
- ☐ Field
- ☐ Hill
- ☐ Rocks
- ☐ Desert

- ☐ Town
- ☐ Railroad
- ☐ Park
- ☐ Airport
- ☐ Museum
- ☐ City

Other features:

_____

_____

**Build** your landscape model using the clay. Then **take a photo** of your finished landscape.

**Draw** a map of your landscape. **Think** about the colors, lines, or symbols you need to add to the map. **Label** any features that need it.

**Discovery** EDUCATION

**Look** at another student's landscape map. What features does this map show?

**Check** all the features you see.

- [ ] Mountain
- [ ] River
- [ ] Valley
- [ ] Lake
- [ ] Road
- [ ] Forest

- [ ] Ocean
- [ ] Stream
- [ ] Field
- [ ] Hill
- [ ] Rocks
- [ ] Desert

- [ ] Town
- [ ] Railroad
- [ ] Park
- [ ] Airport
- [ ] Museum
- [ ] City

Other features:

_____

_____

**Use** the map to **build** a landscape with the clay.

**Think About the Activity**

How did the landscape you made from the map compare to the original landscape?

_____

_____

_____

What was hard about making a map of a landscape?

_____

_____

_____

What was hard about making a landscape from a map?

_____

_____

_____

## How Are Maps Made?

**Read** about maps. **Look** at the pictures.

 **Read Together**

# How Are Maps Made?

### Early Maps

Early explorers made the first maps. They drew pictures to show what they saw. They took these drawings to cartographers. Cartographers were people who drew maps.

Early Map

**SEP** Obtaining, Evaluating, and Communicating Information

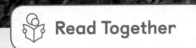 

## Mapping from the Air

As time went on new ways were found to make maps. When airplanes were invented, people used them to help map land.

Coral Reef from the Air

| **Discovery** EDUCATION

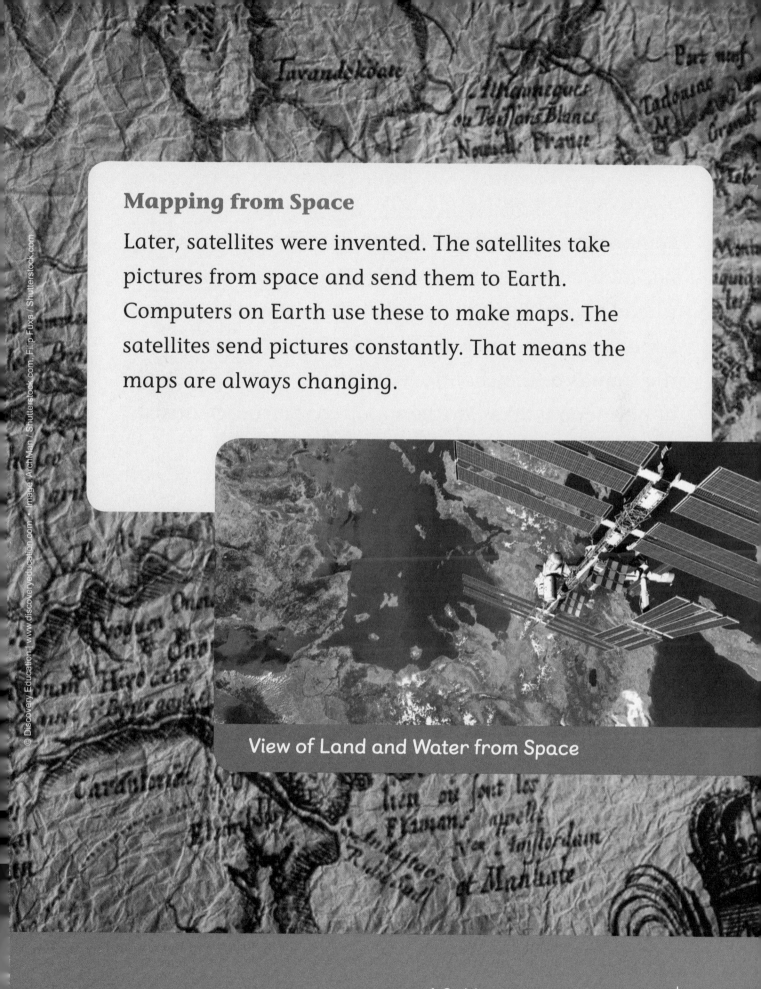

## Mapping from Space

Later, satellites were invented. The satellites take pictures from space and send them to Earth. Computers on Earth use these to make maps. The satellites send pictures constantly. That means the maps are always changing.

View of Land and Water from Space

## Mapping the Seafloor

Some maps need special equipment. The ocean floor has mountains and valleys. We need special equipment to find where they are. Scientists use sonar machines. Sonar machines send signals into the water and record the sounds as they bounce back to the ship. By looking at how long it takes for the sound to return, scientists can make a map of the ocean floor.

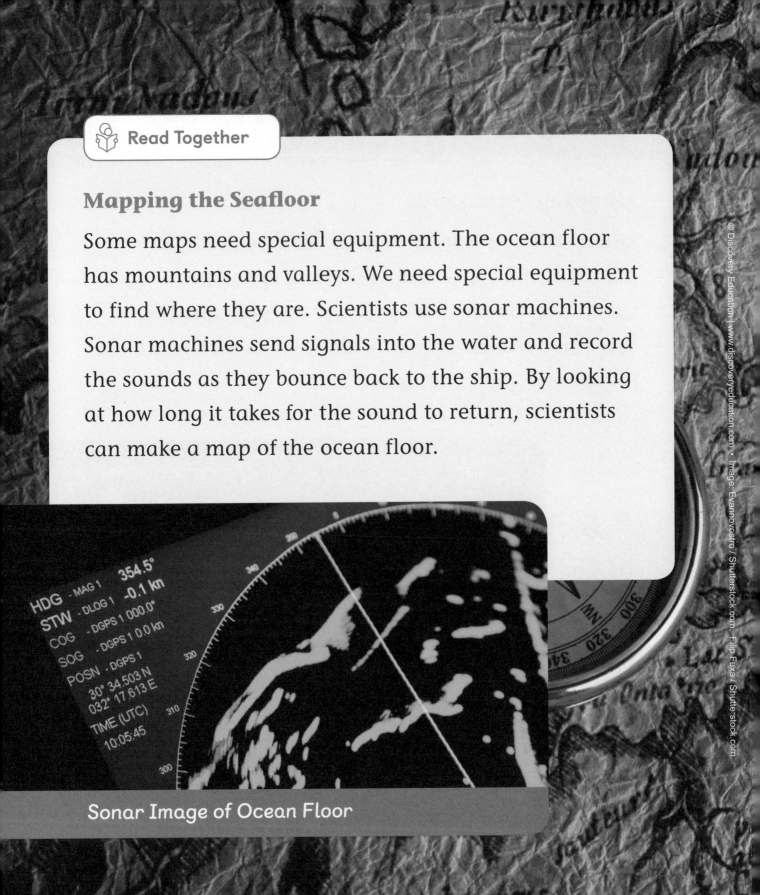

Sonar Image of Ocean Floor

## All Kinds of Maps

There are many kinds of maps, and there are many ways to make them.

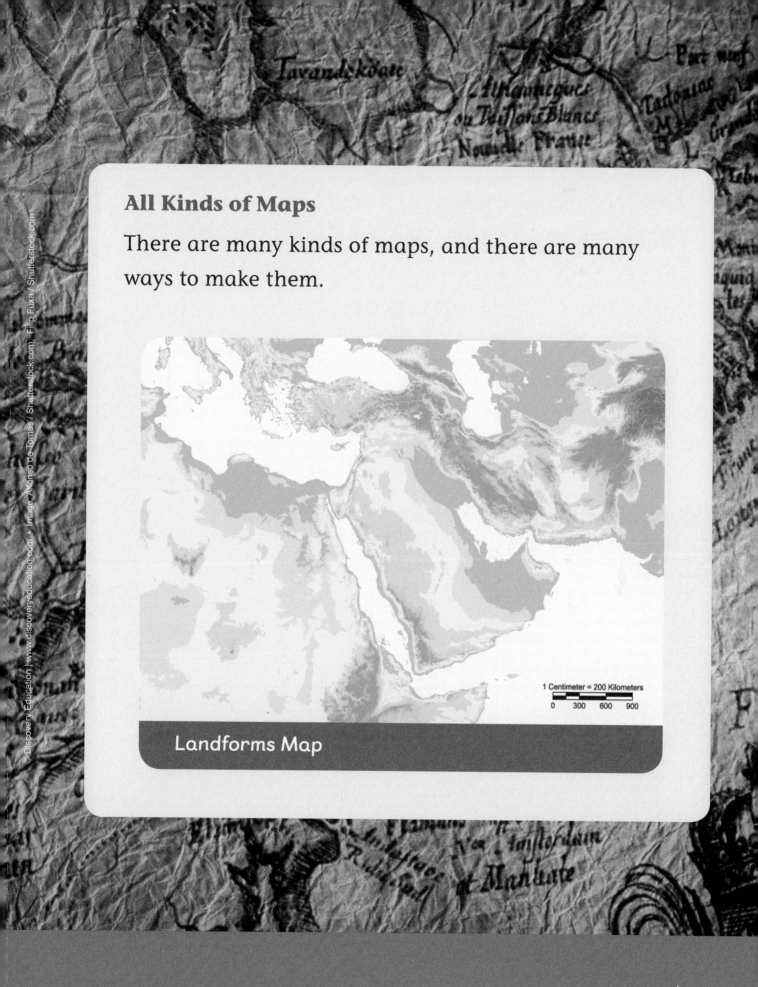

1 Centimeter = 200 Kilometers

0    300    600    900

Landforms Map

**Talk** with a partner about what you learned from the reading. As you share each statement, **place** an X or an O to show you have shared your thinking.

After your partner has shared his or her thinking, **share** a piece of evidence from the reading that connects to his or her thinking.

## XO Let's Go

Quick Code:
ca2052s

**Activity 13**
# Think Like a Scientist

## Use an Image to Make a Map

In this activity, you will use a photo to make a map of a place, such as an island, volcano, mountain, river, or canyon.

**What materials do you need?** (per group)

- Aerial photographs (of a land or water feature such as a river, volcano, island, canyon, mountain, or isthmus)

- Paper
- Colored pencils
- Modeling clay
- Cardboard
- Camera

**SEP**  Developing and Using Models

*Image: Photography by Mangiwau / Moment Open / Getty Images*

*© Discovery Education | www.discoveryeducation.com*

## What Will You Do?

**Look** at some photos. Photos can show the shapes and kinds of land and water in a place.

Islands

Winding River

How do you think these photos were taken?

_____

_____

_____

What land and water features can you see?

_____

_____

_____

**Choose** the materials you will use to make your map.

☐ Paper ☐ Modeling clay

☐ Colored pencils ☐ Cardboard

☐ Markers

**Build** your map using the materials and photo.

**Choose** a landform and photo to model. **Draw** your map. If you used other materials to make your map, **take** a picture of your map.

## Think About the Activity

How is your map like the real world?
How is your map different from the real world?

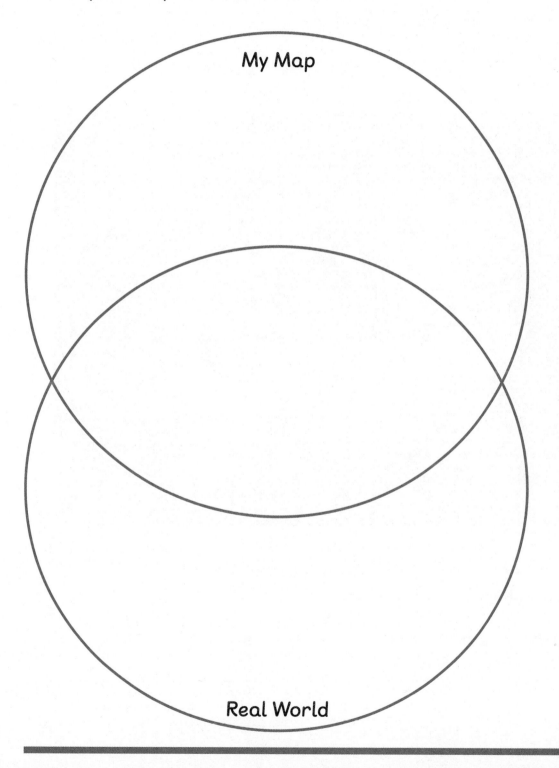

My Map

Real World

**Activity 14**
# Evaluate Like a Scientist

Quick Code:
ca2054s

## Which Map Should I Use?

**Look** at the picture of the model train landscape again.

Model Train Landscape (Bird's Eye View)

What are some different ways a map maker could model this area using maps?

_____

_____

_____

| SEP | Developing and Using Models

© Discovery Education | www.discoveryeducation.com • Image: Rafael Elias / Moment Open / Getty Image. Photography by Mangiwau / Moment Open / Getty Images

**Look** at the maps and the activities. **Match** each activity to the type of map that would best help you.

| Map | Activity |
| --- | --- |

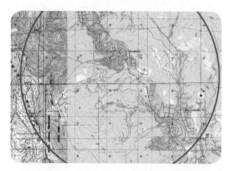

## Why Can a Map Also Be Called a Model?

### Activity 15
# Observe Like a Scientist

Quick Code:
ca2055s

## Models and Maps

**Watch** the video. **Look** for strategies the students use to make their maps.

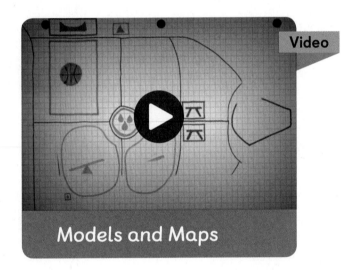

Video

Models and Maps

 Talk Together

Now, talk together about how the students made their map. What did they do first, next, and last?

 **SEP**  Developing and Using Models

## Activity 16
# Think Like a Scientist

Quick Code:
ca2056s

## Map a Park

In this activity, you will make a map to show the natural features of a park.

**What materials do you need?** (per group)

- Paper
- Markers
- Clipboard
- Colored pencils
- Markers

## What Will You Do?

**Go** to a park or outdoor space with your class.

**Look** at the different places or areas in the park. What features will you put on your map?

_____

_____

_____

SEP   Developing and Using Models

**Draw** your map.

**Add** symbols to stand for the different features.

**Discovery**
EDUCATION

**Add** color to your map. How does the color help you read a map?

_____

_____

_____

**Make** a key or legend for your map. What will be in your legend?

| Map Key | |
|---|---|
| **Symbol** | **Meaning** |
| | |
| | |
| | |
| | |

## Think About the Activity

**Compare** your map to others. Do all the maps look alike?

_____

_____

_____

**Think** about what maps tell us about the real world. How can your map help you understand the real world?

_____

_____

_____

**Discovery** EDUCATION

## Activity 17
# Analyze Like a Scientist

Quick Code:
ca2057s

## Models

**Read** about models and **look** at the picture.

 **Read Together**

# Models

Model trains can be a lot of fun. A model train is not the same size as a real train, but it is like a real train in other ways. A model train is shaped like a real train and travels across a landscape in much the same way.

Models can be made of a lot of different things and ideas. Models can also help us think about how we might do a job like putting together a computer. Models can also show us how things like a new building have been put together.

**SEP**  Engaging in Argument from Evidence

**SEP**  Obtaining, Evaluating, and Communicating Information

Maps are models because they show us where things are compared to other things. A map can show where a school is compared to downtown. Maps also show us patterns and how they change, like a weather map does.

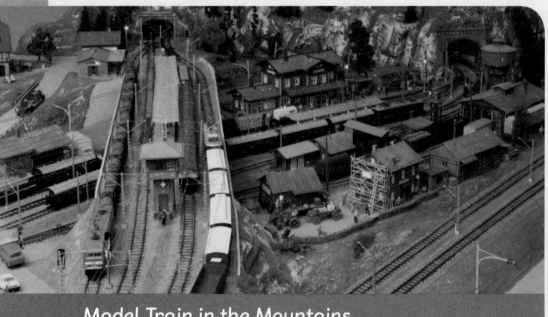

Model Train in the Mountains

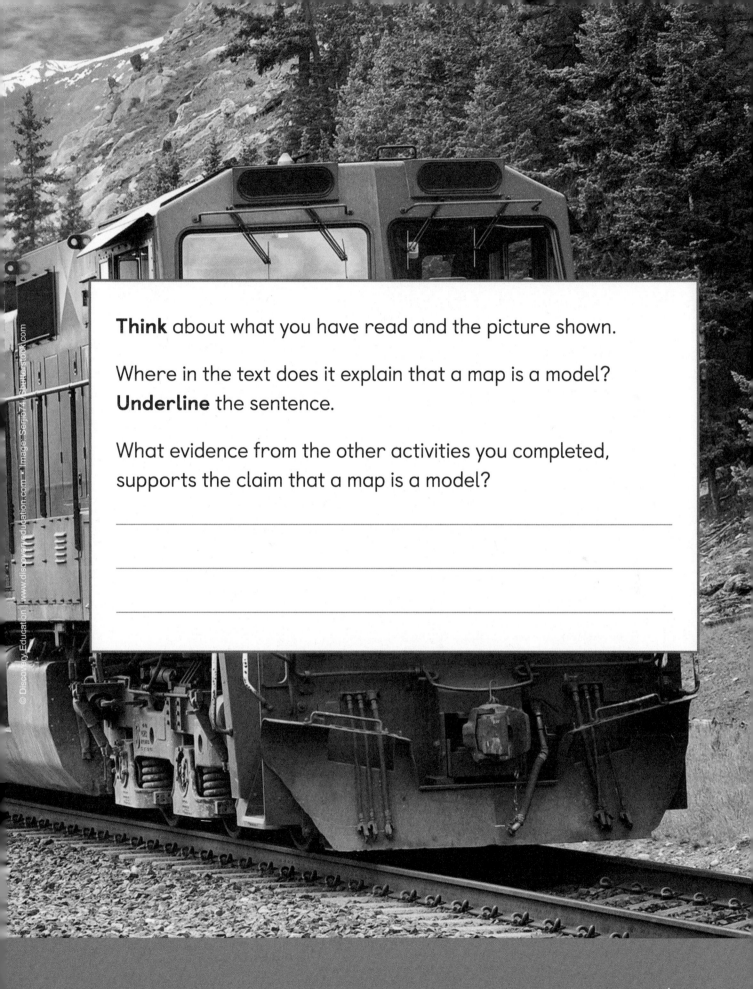

**Think** about what you have read and the picture shown.

Where in the text does it explain that a map is a model?
**Underline** the sentence.

What evidence from the other activities you completed, supports the claim that a map is a model?

_____

_____

_____

**Activity 18**
# Evaluate Like a Scientist

Quick Code:
ca2058s

## Water on a Map

**Look** at the map of Redwood National Park.

How many squares of the grid on the map contain water?

_____

Does the map show more areas of land or water?

_____

**Show** how you found your answer.

| SEP | Using Mathematics and Computational Thinking | | CCC | Patterns |

| SEP | Analyzing and Interpreting Data |

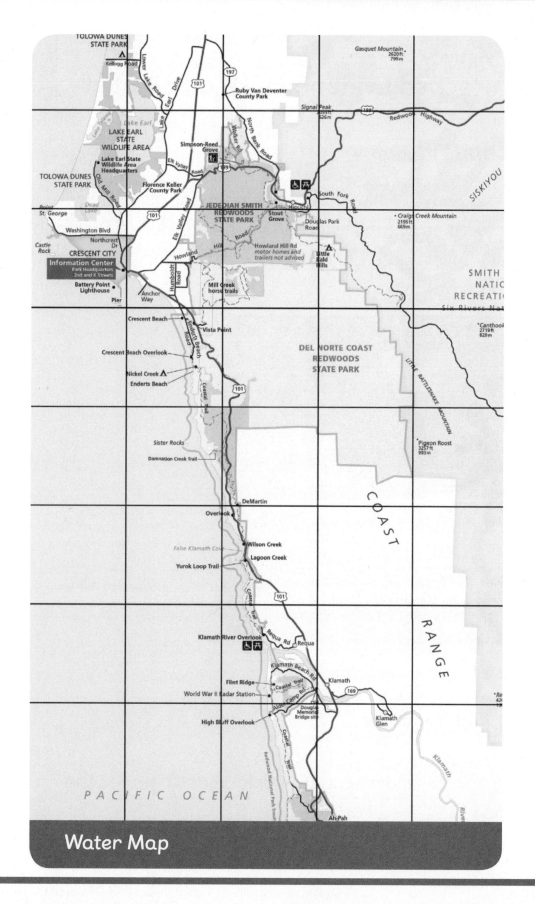

TOLOWA DUNES
STATE PARK

⛺ Kellogg Road

197

Ruby Van Deventer
County Park

Lower Lake Road

Lake Earl Drive

Signal Peak
2035ft
626m

199

Gasquet Mountain
2620ft
799m

Redwoods Highway

*Craigs Creek Mountain*
2195ft
669m

SISKIYOU

*Lake Talawa*

LAKE EARL
STATE
WILDLIFE AREA

Walker Rd

North Bank Road

Simpson-Reed
Grove

● Lake Earl State
Wildlife Area
Headquarters

Elk Valley Road

199

♿ 🏕 Hiouchi

South Fork Road

TOLOWA DUNES
STATE PARK

● Florence Keller
County Park

Old Mill Road

*Dead Lake*

Point
St. George

JEDEDIAH SMITH
REDWOODS
STATE PARK

Stout
Grove

Douglas Park

SMITH
NATIO
RECREATIO

Washington Blvd

Northcrest
Dr

101

Elk Valley Road

Howland Hill Road

Howland Hill Rd
motor homes and
trailers not advised

⛺ Little
Bald
Hills

*Canthook*
2719ft
820m

Six Rivers Nat

Castle
Rock

CRESCENT CITY

Information Center
Park Headquarters
2nd and K Streets

Howland

Humboldt Road

Mill Creek
horse trails

● Battery Point
Lighthouse

Pier

Anchor Way

Crescent Beach ●

Vista Point

Enderts Beach

Crescent Beach Overlook

Nickel Creek ⛺

Enderts Beach

Coastal Trail

101

DEL NORTE COAST
REDWOODS
STATE PARK

LITTLE RATTLESNAKE MOUNTAIN

C

Sister Rocks

Damnation Creek Trail

O

*Pigeon Roost*
3257ft
993m

DeMartin

A

Overlook

*False Klamath Cove*

● Wilson Creek

● Lagoon Creek

Yurok Loop Trail

S

101

Coastal Trail

Requa Rd

T

Klamath River Overlook ♿ 🏕

Requa

R

Flint Ridge

Klamath Beach Rd

Coastal Trail

● Klamath

169

World War II Radar Station

Alder Camp Rd

A

*Re*
420

High Bluff Overlook

Douglas
Memorial
Bridge site

N

Klamath
Glen

Coastal Trail

Redwood National Park boundary

G

Klamath River

PACIFIC OCEAN

E

Ah-Pah

## Water Map

**Activity 19**
# Record Evidence Like a Scientist

Quick Code:
ca2059s

## Landscapes in Animation

Now that you have learned about using maps as models to show the location of landforms and water features, look again at the Let's Investigate Landscapes in Animation. You first saw this in Wonder.

Let's Investigate Landscapes in Animation

**Talk Together**

How do you think landscapes in animations help tell the story now?

SEP **Constructing Explanations and Designing Solutions**

**Look** at the Can You Explain? question. You first read this question at the beginning of the lesson.

## Can You Explain?

How can you show the location of landforms and water features?

**Read** the example of the start of a scientific explanation.
**Complete** each statement.

**Claim:** A _____ is a model that can show the location of landforms and water features.

**Evidence:** I observed _____

_____

**Reasoning:** Since a _____ shows the _____ of real-world objects in comparison to the _____ of other real-world objects, a map can help you locate landforms and water features. A map can be used to _____ where things are located.

Now, you will use your new ideas about Let's Investigate Landscapes in Animation to answer a question.

1. **Choose** a question. You can use the Can You Explain? question, or one of your own. You can also use one of the questions that you wrote at the beginning of the lesson.

**Your Questions**

2. Then, **use** these sentence starters to answer the question.

A map is a model that can show

_____

_____

Relief maps can show

_____

_____

_____

© Discovery Education | www.discoveryeducation.com • Image: Photography by Mangwau / Moment Open / Getty Images

**Discovery** EDUCATION

Other maps like topographic maps

_____

_____

_____

Landmarks on a map can be

_____

_____

Color can help you

_____

_____

Water features

_____

_____

A legend is

_____

_____

_____

# STEM in Action

Quick Code:
ca2060s

Activity 20
## Analyze Like a Scientist

Museum Models

**Read** the story.

 Read Together

# Museum Models

Making **model** landscapes is not just something you do in school. Museum exhibit designers often plan landscape displays. These displays are models that show the setting of events in history.

Museum Landscape
Display

| SEP | Analyzing and Interpreting Data | CCC | Scale, Proportion, and Quantity |

  **Discovery**
EDUCATION

Designers try to make the displays as realistic as possible. When you look into the glass case, you can see a miniature scene from history!

Video

Yosemite Visitor Center

If you were an exhibit designer for the Yosemite Visitor's Center, how could you use what you have learned so far in this unit to make displays?

_____

_____

_____

_____

# Mountains

**Look** at this map of California. Where does the map show mountains? **Circle** the mountains.

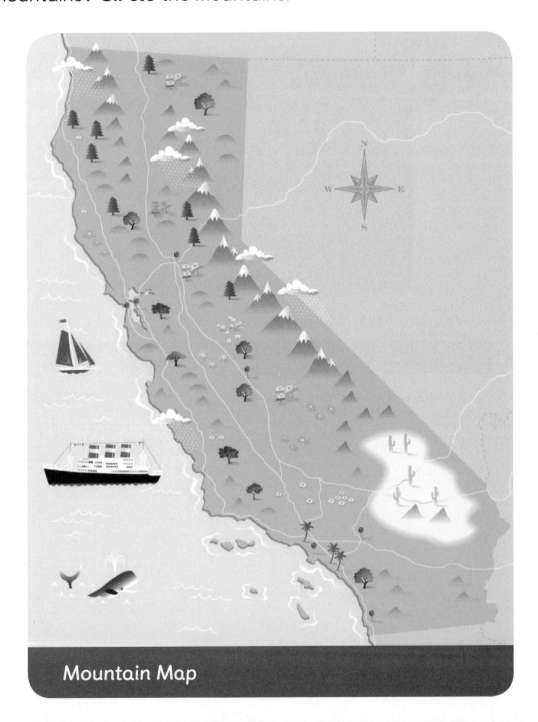

Mountain Map

## Activity 21
## Evaluate Like a Scientist

Quick Code:
ca2061s

### Review: Mapping Landscapes

**Think** about what you have read and seen. What did you learn?

**Draw** what you have learned. Then, **tell** someone else about what you learned.

**Talk Together**

Think about what you saw in Get Started. Use your new ideas to discuss mapping landscapes.

SEP  Developing and Using Models

# Land and Water Relationships

## Student Objectives

By the end of this lesson:

☐ I can use evidence and patterns to predict where to find water on Earth.

☐ I can use models to show how bodies of water go together to make a larger water system.

☐ I can use maps to put together information about the land and water in an area.

## Key Vocabulary

☐ drought

☐ fresh water

☐ survive

Quick Code:
ca2065s

### Activity 1
## Can You Explain?

How do maps show relationships between water and land?

_____

_____

_____

_____

_____

Quick Code:
ca2066s

**Discovery** EDUCATION

Whitney
Las Vegas
Mead
Hoover Dam
Death Valley
Henderson
Colorado
Kingman
Barstow
San Bernardino
Joshua Tree National Park
Riverside
Escondido
Yuma

### Activity 2
# Ask Questions Like a Scientist

Quick Code:
ca2067s

## Drought

**Look** at the photo. **Answer** the questions.

Let's Investigate Drought

What do you think happened to this field of plants?

_____

_____

_____

What happened to the water? Where did the water go? **Use** the chart to **write** your ideas.

| Drought | |
|---|---|
| I see . . . | |
| I think . . . | |
| I wonder . . . | |

What questions do you have about drought?

**Your Questions**

# Water on Earth

You can get thirsty after playing outside. You should drink some water soon after playing. Living things need water to **survive**. Without water, they will die.

Some areas on Earth have a lot of water. Other areas do not. Areas that do not have enough water experience **drought**.

**Drinking Water**

We use water every day. Think about how much water you use. Now think about where all the water you use comes from.

© Discovery Education | www.discoveryeducation.com • Image: khak / Shutterstock.com; vystekimages / Shutterstock.com. Icon: Freepik from www.flaticon.com

## Activity 3
# Analyze Like a Scientist

## Water on Earth

Do you ever wonder where water comes from?
**Add** some more questions to your chart.

| Drought | |
|---|---|
| I wonder . . . | |

### Activity 4
# Observe Like a Scientist

Quick Code:
ca2069s

## Children Playing

**Look** at the picture of these children playing. Do you think they will get thirsty?

**Children Playing**

Where on Earth do you find water?

_____

_____

### Activity 5
# Observe Like a Scientist

Quick Code:
ca2070s

## Using Water

**Watch** the video. **Look** for ways people use water.

Using Water

 **Talk Together**

Now, talk together about ways that you have used water today. How many different ways did you use water today?

**Activity 6**
# Observe Like a Scientist

Quick Code:
ca2071s

## Earth's Water

**Watch** the video. **Look** for water in liquid and solid form.

Earth's Water

 **Talk Together**

Now, talk together about different places solid and liquid water are found.

Quick Code: ca2072s

## Activity 7
# Evaluate Like a Scientist

## What Do You Already Know About Land and Water Relationships?

**Making the Match**

Earth has water and land. **Look** at each picture. **Match** it to the correct word on the right.

| Image | Description |
|-------|-------------|

**Image**

**Description**

River

Marsh

Lake

**SEP** Developing and Using Models

### Where Is the Water?

**Look** at the different places. Which ones have water?
Put a check next to all of the places that have water.

 ☐

 ☐

 ☐

 ☐

  ☐

## Parts of a Map

**Look** at the map. **Match** each of the parts of the map to the thing that they stand for in the real world. For example, the red lines show the state boundary.

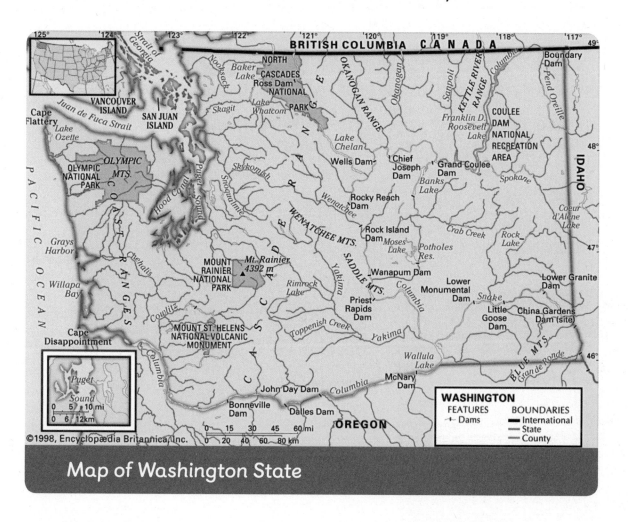

Map of Washington State

| Part of Map | Stands For |
|---|---|
| Blue lines | Ocean water |
| Green shaded area | Rivers and streams |
| Light blue shaded area | Forests or parks |

# Find the Water

Water can be found all over Earth. Water can be found as ice or as a liquid. In fact, about 70 percent of Earth's surface is covered with water. That means 30 percent of the surface is land.

Look at a globe. Some areas are covered by land, and some are covered by water. Think about what would happen if you put on a blindfold, spun the globe, and placed your index finger in a random spot. Sometimes your index finger would be on a water feature and sometimes it would be on a landform.

Exploring a Globe

# Where Is Water Found on Earth?

 **Activity 8**
## Analyze Like a Scientist

Quick Code:
ca2075s

### Find the Water

**Spin** a globe. With your eyes closed, **point** to the globe. **Write** down what you point to, land or water. **Do** this task ten times.

How many times did your index finger point to a water feature? How many times did it point to a landform?

**CCC** Scale, Proportion, and Quantity

**Activity 9**
## Observe Like a Scientist

Quick Code:
ca2076s

## Waters of Earth

Most of Earth is covered with water. Rivers, streams, lakes, and ponds hold Earth's **fresh water**. Oceans and seas contain salt water. There is even some water underground!

**Watch** and **complete** the Interactive. **Look** at the different bodies of water on Earth.

Waters of Earth

CCC   **Patterns**

Discovery
EDUCATION

**Draw** a body of water near where you live. **Label** it.

**Explore** the different bodies of water found on Earth.
**Write** your observations in the table.

| Data | | |
|---|---|---|
| Water Body | Type of Water | |
| | | |
| | | |
| | | |
| | | |
| | | |
| | | |

| Data | | |
|---|---|---|
| | Where It Forms | Other Information |
| | | |
| | | |
| | | |
| | | |
| | | |

**Activity 10**
# Think Like a Scientist

Quick Code:
ca2077s

## Land and Water

Water can be found all over Earth. Water can be found as ice or as a liquid. In this activity, you will make a model to compare the amount of land to the amount of water on Earth.

**What materials do you need?** (per group)

- Measuring cups
- Modeling clay
- Pitcher
- Paper
- Crayons

**SEP** Developing and Using Models

**CCC** Scale, Proportion, and Quantity

## What Will You Do?

You can show fractions using a fraction strip. The strip has four parts that make up a whole. **Shade** three parts of the fraction strip.

What fraction of the strip is shaded?

**Use** a measuring cup to model the land and water on Earth.
**Fill** the measuring cup with clay to represent the amount of land on Earth.

**Pour** water in to fill the rest of the measuring cup.

**Draw** your model.

Discovery
E D U C A T I O N

**Think About the Activity**

How does your model show Earth's water and land?

_____

_____

_____

What fraction of Earth's surface is covered by water?

_____

_____

What fraction of Earth's surface is covered by land?

_____

_____

# Bodies of Water

Oceans cover most of Earth's surface. They are the largest bodies of water on Earth. Oceans are filled with salt water.

**Hallstatt Lake**

A lake is a large body of water with land around it. Lakes provide food and water to animals and people. Most of the water found in lakes is fresh water.

Fresh water flows into the ocean from rivers and streams. The Amazon and the Nile are the two largest rivers on Earth.

Glaciers are large, slow rivers of ice. As glaciers move, they change the land. Think about what the weather could be like in places where there are glaciers.

# Analyze Like a Scientist

Quick Code:
ca2078s

## Bodies of Water

**Write** in the chart to tell about each body of water.
**Tell** if the body of water is *solid* or *liquid* water.

| Body of Water | Description | Solid or Liquid? |
| --- | --- | --- |
| Ocean | | |
| Lake | | |
| River | | |
| Glacier | | |

# Water World

Look at this map of the world. The blue parts of the map show where there is water. The white parts show where ice covers land. The parts that are green and brown show where there is land. Most of the blue on the map shows where there are oceans.

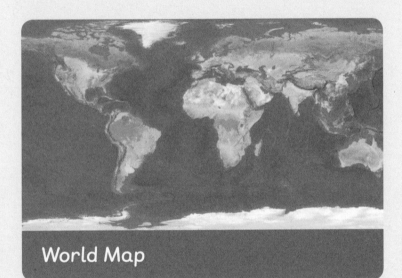

World Map

Water is a natural resource. A tree is a natural resource on land. Think about what other natural resources help us survive.

## Activity 12
# Analyze Like a Scientist

Quick Code:
ca2079s

## Water World

**Review** the different types of Earth's water features you have learned about.

Is there more water or land on the map? Are there other kinds of water that you don't see on the map?

_____

_____

_____

_____

_____

### Activity 13
# Evaluate Like a Scientist

Quick Code:
ca2080s

## Land and Water

**Look** at this picture of Earth. **Write** the correct words on the map to tell whether the areas are land or water.

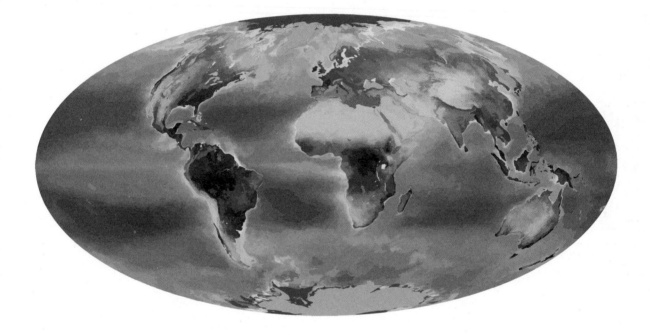

**CCC**   Scale, Proportion, and Quantity

**Discovery**
EDUCATION

How can you recognize water on a map? How can you recognize land?

_____

_____

**Draw** to show a fraction that stands for the amount of water and land on Earth.

# How Are Bodies of Water Connected?

### Activity 14
## Observe Like a Scientist

Quick Code:
ca2081s

## Map of Washington State

**Look** at the map. **Trace** the path of some rivers with a marker.

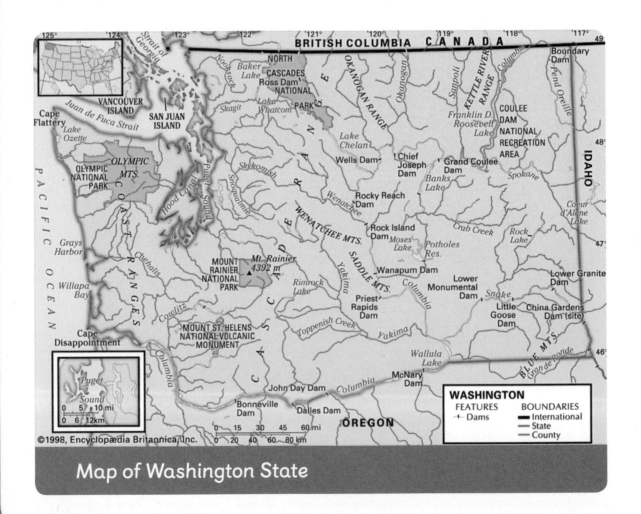

Map of Washington State

## Activity 15
# Observe Like a Scientist

Quick Code: ca2082s

## Rivers and Streams

**Watch** the video about rivers and streams. **Look** for the differences between a river and lake. Find out about watersheds.

Video

Rivers and Streams

**Talk Together**

Now, talk together about the change in elevation at the start and end of a stream. How does a stream change from beginning to end?

# Connecting Bodies of Water

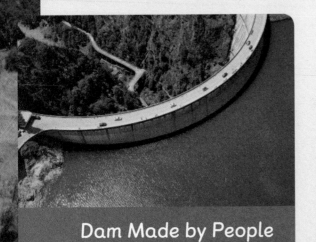

Dam Made by People

All water flows toward lower ground. Water from lakes, streams, and rivers flow toward lower ground and into the ocean. Dams, made by both beavers and humans, can change the flow of water.

Beaver Dam

## Connecting Bodies of Water

What happens when a dam is placed in the river?

_____

_____

_____

_____

_____

### Activity 17
# Think Like a Scientist

Quick Code:
ca2084s

## Mapping Rivers

In this activity, you will **look** at a map of your state and **trace** the flow of rivers.

**What materials do you need?** (per group)

- Reference map of your state
- Rivers and lakes map of your state
- Computer access
- Colored pencils
- Red pencils
- Green pencils

What state do you live in? **Draw** or **write** your answer.

© Discovery Education | www.discoveryeducation.com • Image: Bill Swindaman / Moment / Getty Images

**SEP** Obtaining, Evaluating, and Communicating Information

## What Will You Do?

**Look** at this picture of streams, a river, and a lake.

**Trace** the way the water flows.

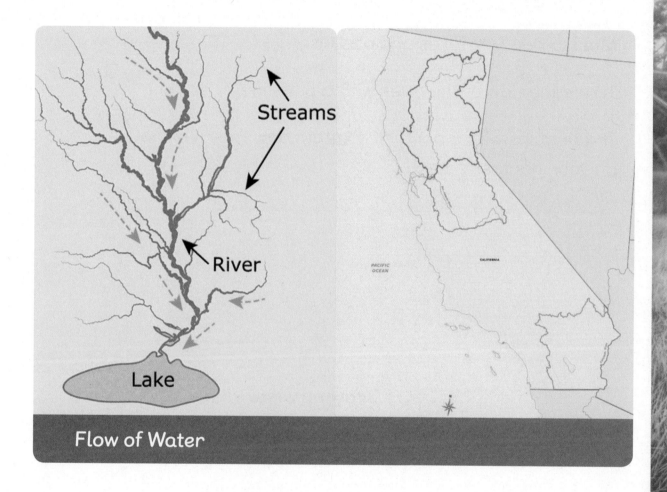

**Get** a map of your state. **Find** the rivers on it.

**Look** for where a river starts. **Mark** a green X where each river starts. **Look** for mountains if you are not sure.

**Mark** a red X on lakes and oceans.

**Trace** the flow of the river with a blue line.

**Trade** maps with a partner. **Explain** how the river flows on your partner's map.

_____

_____

_____

_____

© Discovery Education | www.discoveryeducation.com • Image: Bill Swindaman / Moment / Getty Images

**Discovery** EDUCATION

## Think About the Activity

**Think** about the ways that streams and rivers flow. Where do they start? Where do they end?

**Fill in** the flowchart to answer the questions.

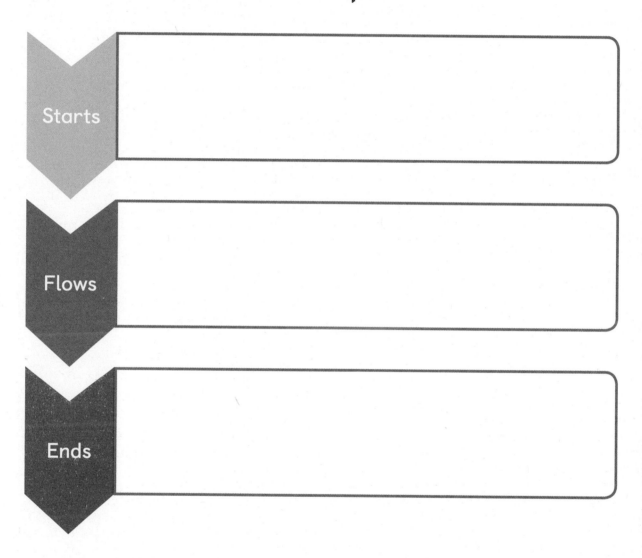

Starts

Flows

Ends

What is important about rivers?

_____

_____

_____

_____

What can you do to help rivers?

_____

_____

_____

_____

# How Can Maps Be Used to Answer Questions About How Land and Water Are Connected?

**Activity 18**
## Observe Like a Scientist

Quick Code: ca2085s

## Mountain Scene

**Look** at the picture of this mountain. What different forms of water do you see? **Circle** them in the picture.

Mountain Scene

Quick Code:
ca2086s

## Using Maps

**Read** the story. Then, **answer** the questions.

 **Read Together**

# Using Maps

Maps are tools that help us answer questions. Where is the best place to live in the state of California? A map of California could help you answer this question. If you like to swim, you might live near a lake or the ocean. If you want to farm, you might live on flat land in the valley. Do you like snow? You might like to live in the mountains.

Maps can help answer another question. Streams, rivers, lakes, and oceans are water features often marked on a map. But there is one more source of water you may not know.

Map of California

Mountains are landforms that are also a water source. As you travel up a mountain, the air gets more moisture. Moist air brings rain. The higher you go, the colder the air gets. The rain turns to snow. When the snow melts, it flows down the mountain into rivers and lakes.

As you read this last paragraph, **draw** what you think it is describing.

How does the Mountain Scene picture you saw in Activity 18 relate to the steps you just read about?

_____

_____

_____

_____

What would happen to a farmer if one year there was not a lot of snow?

_____

_____

_____

_____

## Activity 20
# Evaluate Like a Scientist

Quick Code:
ca2087s

## How Does Water Flow?

What are the steps water takes to travel from the mountains to the ocean? The pictures are not in the correct order. **Number** the pictures from one to five to show the correct order of how water flows.

**CCC** Systems and System Models

**Activity 21**
# Record Evidence Like a Scientist

Quick Code:
ca2088s

## Drought

Now that you have learned more about how water and land are related, look again at the Let's Investigate Drought image. You first saw this in Wonder.

Let's Investigate Drought

**Talk Together**

How do you think drought helps you understand more about where water comes from?

SEP   **Constructing Explanations and Designing Solutions**

**Look** at the Can You Explain? question. You first read this question at the beginning of the lesson.

>  **Can You Explain?**
>
> How do maps show relationships between water and land?

Now, you will use your new ideas about Let's Investigate Drought to answer a question.

1. **Choose** a question. You can use the Can You Explain? question, or one of your own. You can also use one of the questions that you wrote at the beginning of the lesson.

**Your Question**

2. Then, **use** the sentence starters on the next page to answer the question.

When I looked at maps, I observed patterns

_____

_____

I also saw that maps use colors to show

_____

_____

When I looked at a map that showed mountains, I saw

_____

_____

When I traced the rivers on different maps, I saw that streams start

_____

and flow

_____

that flow

_____

I think that patterns on maps do show

_____

_____

_____

# STEM in Action

**Activity 22**

## Analyze Like a Scientist

### Creating Farms

**Read** the story. **Circle** the sentence that tells how farmers use maps.

 **Read Together**

# Creating Farms

Farming is important for growing all types of food. Farmers know that their farms need to be built near water to help the crops grow. Farmers use maps to help them build their farm. These maps show the land and water. A map that shows the land and water helps farmers figure out how much water they will have.

North Dakota has many farms. Farms there grow corn, soybeans, and other crops.

**SEP** Obtaining, Evaluating, and Communicating Information

## Map of North Dakota

**Look** at the map of North Dakota.

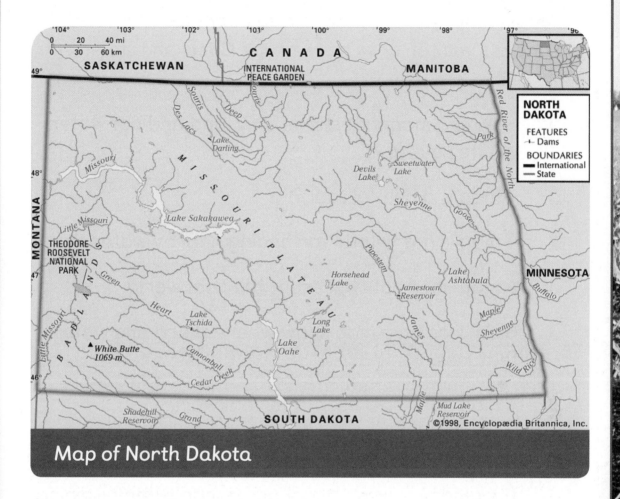

Map of North Dakota

What evidence from the map helps you predict if North Dakota has a lot of drought?

_____

_____

## Farming for a Day

**Imagine** that you are a farmer. You want to make your farm bigger so you can grow more crops. **Check** the statements below that are true.

❑ Having a map that shows only land and not water will be helpful.

❑ A map is a helpful tool.

❑ A map is not helpful for finding nearby water.

❑ A map does not represent the real world.

❑ Blue lines on a map show where there are water features.

❑ A map does represent the real world.

❑ A map shows where there are nearby towns.

❑ It would be easier to not use a map when planning to make a bigger farm.

❑ A map can show the land and water in an area.

❑ A map might show the type of soil in an area.

## Activity 23
# Evaluate Like a Scientist

Quick Code:
ca2092s

## Review: Land and Water Relationships

**Think** about what you have read and seen. What did you learn?

**Draw** what you have learned. Then, tell someone else about what you learned.

### Talk Together

Think about what you saw in Get Started. Use your new ideas to discuss how land and water are related.

SEP  Developing and Using Models

# Unit Project

 **Design Solutions Like a Scientist**

Quick Code:
ca2093s

## Hands-On Engineering: Capturing Runoff from Landscapes

In this activity, you will make a landscape that shows how runoff water can be captured and collected. You will then tell how the captured runoff can help a place that has drought.

Water Runoff

### Ask Questions About the Problem

What is the problem you are trying to solve?

_____

_____

_____

**What materials do you need?** (per group)

- Modeling clay
- Aluminum foil pan, 13×9×2
- Pitcher
- Water
- Soil, potting
- Kinetic sand
- Craft sticks
- String
- Plastic bottle, 8 oz
- Waxed paper cup, 200 mL

## What Will You Do?

**Think** about what you learned about the shape of land and how water relates to it. **Brainstorm** ideas on how you can solve the problem.

_____

_____

_____

What materials will you use for the runoff capture system?

_____

_____

_____

| SEP | Developing and Using Models |
| SEP | Constructing Explanations and Designing Solutions |
| CCC | Patterns |
| CCC | Systems and System Models |

**Make** your landscape. Then **design** and **build** your runoff capture system.

How will you know if your design can capture runoff?

_____

_____

_____

_____

**Test** your design. **Draw** or **write** to show how you tested it.

**Think About the Activity**

**Write** or **draw** your answers to the questions in the chart.

How well did your design collect water?

How could you improve your design?

| What Worked? | What Didn't Work? |
|---|---|
| | |

**What Could Work Better?**

# Grade 2 Resources

- Bubble Map
- Safety in the Science Classroom
- Vocabulary Flash Cards
- Glossary
- Index

**Name** _____

# Bubble Map

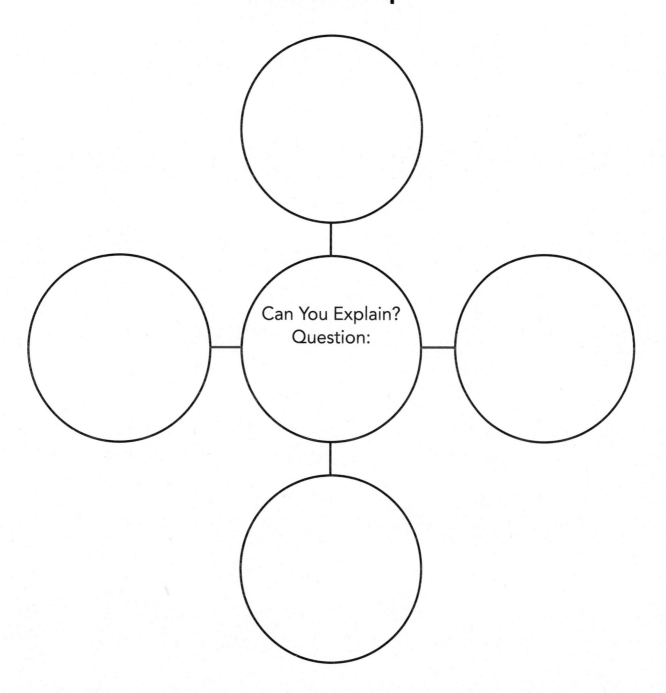

Can You Explain?
Question:

Following common safety practices is the first rule of any laboratory or field scientific investigation.

## Dress for Safety

One of the most important steps in a safe investigation is dressing appropriately.

- Splash goggles need to be kept on during the entire investigation.

- Use gloves to protect your hands when handling chemicals or organisms.

- Tie back long hair to prevent it from coming in contact with chemicals or a heat source.

- Wear proper clothing and clothing protection. Roll up long sleeves, and if they are available, wear a lab coat or apron over your clothes. Always wear closed-toe shoes. During field investigations, wear long pants and long sleeves.

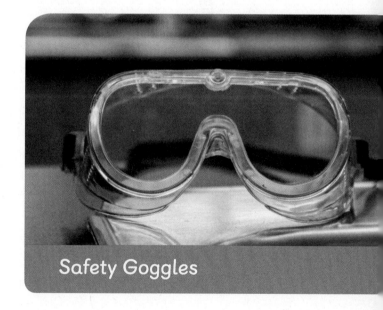

Safety Goggles

## Be Prepared for Accidents

Even if you are practicing safe behavior during an investigation, accidents can happen. Learn the emergency equipment location in your classroom and how to use it.

- The eye and face wash station can help if a harmful substance or foreign object gets into your eyes or onto your face.

- Fire blankets and fire extinguishers can be used to smother and put out fires in the laboratory. Talk to your teacher about fire safety in the lab. He or she may not want you to directly handle the fire blanket and fire extinguisher. However, you should still know where these items are in case the teacher asks you to retrieve them.

Fire Extinguisher

Most importantly, when an accident occurs, immediately alert your teacher and classmates. Do not try to keep the accident a secret or respond to it by yourself. Your teacher and classmates can help you.

# Practice Safe Behavior

There are many ways to stay safe during a scientific investigation. You should always use safe and appropriate behavior before, during, and after your investigation.

- Read all of the steps of the procedure before beginning your investigation. Make sure you understand all the steps. Ask your teacher for help if you do not understand any part of the procedure.

- Gather all your materials and keep your workstation neat and organized. Label any chemicals you are using.

- During the investigation, be sure to follow the steps of the procedure exactly. Use only directions and materials that have been approved by your teacher.

- Eating and drinking are not allowed during an investigation. If asked to observe the odor of a substance, do so using the correct procedure known as wafting, in which you cup your hand over the container holding the substance and gently wave enough air toward your face to make sense of the smell.

- When performing investigations, stay focused on the steps of the procedure and your behavior during the investigation. During investigations, there are many materials and equipment that can cause injuries.

- Treat animals and plants with respect during an investigation.

- After the investigation is over, appropriately dispose of any chemicals or other materials that you have used. Ask your teacher if you are unsure of how to dispose of anything.

- Make sure that you have returned any extra materials and pieces of equipment to the correct storage space.

- Leave your workstation clean and neat. Wash your hands thoroughly.

**Discovery** EDUCATION

## canyon

Image: Galen Rowell / Corbis Documentary / Getty Images

a deep valley that has very steep sides

## characteristic

Image: Paul Fuqua

a special quality that something may have

## drought

Image: Inga Spence / Photolibrary / Getty Images

when there is no rain for a long period

## elevation

Image: MollieGPhoto

the height of an area of land above sea level

## feature

Image: Ocean First Education

a thing that describes what something looks like; part of something

## fresh water

Image: NASA

water that is not salty, such as that found in streams and lakes

## landform

Image: Paul Fuqua

a feature of Earth that has been formed by nature, such as a hill or a valley

## landscape

Image: Paul Fuqua

the view of a land's surface

## location

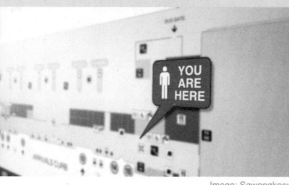

Image: Sawangkaew

a place where something is

## map

Image: U.S.D.A. Forest Service

a flat picture or drawing of a place that is made to show things such as streets or towns in an area

## model

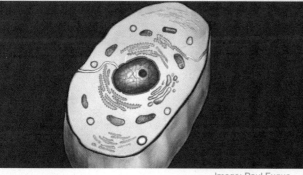

Image: Paul Fuqua

a human-made version created to show the parts of something else either big or small

## mountain

Image: Paul Fuqua

a very tall area of land that is higher than a hill and has steep sides

## naturalist

Image: Prachaya Roekdeethaweesab

someone who studies nature, especially plants and animals

## ocean

Image: Paul Fuqua

a large body of salt water

## plain

Image: Discovery Education

a large flat area of land without trees

## plateau

Image: AnilD / Shutterstock.com

a large, flat area of land that is higher than the other land around it

## preserve

Image: Paul Fuqua

to protect or keep
something safe

## quadrilateral

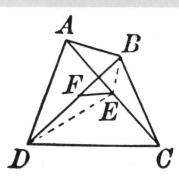

Image: Morphart Creation / Shutterstock.com

a flat shape with four straight
sides, such as a square or a
parallelogram

## relief map

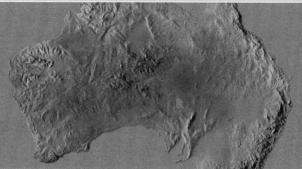

Image: Discovery Education

a type of map that shows how
flat or steep the landforms are
in an area

## river

Image: Paul Fuqua

water flowing through a
landscape, usually fed by
smaller streams

## slope

Image: Discovery Communications, Inc.

land that is slanted or angles downward

## stream

Image: Paul Fuqua

a small flowing body of water that starts with a spring and ends at a river

## survive

Image: Paul Fuqua

to continue to live

## two-dimensional

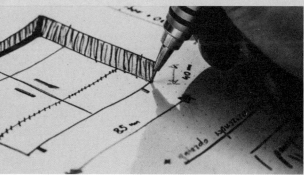

Image: Pixabay

drawings and sketches that are done on flat paper to show width and height

# valley

Image: Paul Fuqua

the low place between two
hills or mountains

## English ——— A ——— Español

**absorb**
to take in or soak up

**absorber**
tomar o captar

**absorption**
how much something can take in and hold

**absorción**
cuanto algo puede tomar y retener

**adjust**
to fix or change something

**ajustar**
arreglar o cambiar algo

**analyze**
to closely examine something and then explain it

**analizar**
examinar con atención algo y luego explicarlo

## ——— B ———

**barrier**
something that is used to stop or block materials from moving

**barrera**
algo que se usa para evitar o bloquear el movimiento de materiales

**biodiversity**

the many different types of life that live together in an environment

**biodiversidad**

muchos y diferentes tipos de vida que conviven en un medio ambiente

— C —

**canyon**

a deep valley that has very steep sides

**cañón**

valle profundo que tiene laderas muy pronunciadas

**channel**

a path that is dug and used for drainage or protection against things like water, mud, or rocks

**canal**

vía cavada que se usa como desagüe o protección contra cosas como el agua, el lodo o las rocas

**characteristic**

a special quality that something may have

**característica**

cualidad especial que tiene algo

— D —

**dissolve**

to mix something with a liquid, such as water, so that it can't be seen anymore

**disolver**

mezclar algo con un líquido, como el agua, de manera que no se pueda ver más

**drought**
when there is no rain for a
long period

**sequía**
cuando no llueve durante un
período prolongado

—————— E ——————

**Earth's crust**
the top layer of Earth that is the
thinnest and the most important
because it is where we live

**corteza de la Tierra**
capa superior de la Tierra que es la
más delgada y la más importante
porque allí es donde vivimos

**earthquake**
a sudden shaking of the ground
caused by the movement of rock
underground

**terremoto**
repentina sacudida de la tierra
causada por el movimiento de
roca subterránea

**elevation**
the height of an area of land
above sea level

**elevación**
altura de un área de tierra por
encima del nivel del mar

**engineer**
a person who designs something
that may be helpful to solve a
problem

**ingeniero**
persona que diseña algo que
puede ser útil para resolver un
problema

**engineering**

using math and science to design and build machines, structures, and other devices

**ingenería**

usar las matemáticas y las ciencias para diseñar y construir máquinas, estructuras y otros dispositivos

---

**environment**

all the living and nonliving things that surround an organism

**medio ambiente**

todos los seres vivos y objetos sin vida que rodean a un organismo

---

**erosion**

when soil is moved from one location to another by wind or water

**erosión**

cuando el viento o el agua transporta suelo de un lugar a otro

---

**estimate**

to make a careful guess

**estimar**

hacer una suposición consciente

--- F ---

**feature**

a thing that describes what something looks like; part of something

**rasgo**

cosa que describe cómo se ve algo; parte de algo

**flexibility**
the ability to bend without breaking

**flexibilidad**
capacidad de doblarse sin romperse

**fresh water**
water that is not salty, such as that found in streams and lakes

**agua dulce**
agua que no es salada, como la que se encuentra en arroyos y lagos

## G

**gemstone**
a colorful stone found in nature that can be used for jewelry

**piedra preciosa**
piedra colorida que se encuentra en la naturaleza y se puede usar para hacer joyas

## H

**habitat**
the place where a plant or animal lives

**hábitat**
lugar donde vive una planta o un animal

**hardness**
a measure of how difficult it is to scratch a mineral: Diamonds are the hardest mineral. They have a hardness scale rating of 10.

**dureza**
medida de cuán difícil es rayar un material: los diamantes son los minerales más duros. Su clasificación en la escala de dureza es 10.

## L

**landfill**
a place where trash is buried

**vertedero**
lugar donde se entierra la basura

**landform**
a feature of Earth that has been formed by nature, such as a hill or a valley

**accidente geográfico**
característica de la Tierra formada por la naturaleza, como una colina o un valle

**landscape**
the view of a land's surface

**paisaje**
vista de la superficie de un terreno

**location**
a place where something is

**ubicación**
lugar donde se encuentra algo

## M

**map**
a flat picture or drawing of a place that is made to show things, such as streets or towns, in an area

**mapa**
imagen o dibujo plano de un lugar que se hace para mostrar cosas, como las calles o las ciudades, de un área

**material**

things that can be used to build or create something

**material**

cosas que se pueden usar para construir o crear algo

---

**matter**

the things around you that take up space like solids, liquids, and gases

**materia**

cosas que nos rodean y ocupan espacio, como los sólidos, los líquidos y los gases

---

**mixture**

a combination of different things, but you can pick out each different one

**mezcla**

combinación de diferentes cosas, pero se puede identificar cada una

---

**model**

a human-made version created to show the parts of something else, either big or small

**modelo**

versión creada por el hombre para mostrar las partes de algo más, ya sea grande o pequeño

---

**mountain**

a very tall area of land that is higher than a hill and has steep sides

**montaña**

área de tierra muy alta que es más alta que una colina y tiene laderas pronunciadas

## N

**naturalist**
someone who studies nature, especially plants and animals

**naturalista**
alguien que estudia la naturaleza, especialmente las plantas y los animales

**nutrient**
something in food that helps people, animals, and plants live and grow

**nutriente**
algo en los alimentos que ayuda a las personas, los animales y las plantas a vivir y crecer

## O

**observe**
to watch closely

**observar**
mirar atentamente

**ocean**
a large body of salt water

**océano**
gran cuerpo de agua salada

**organism**
a living thing

**organismo**
ser vivo

## P

**plain**
a large flat area of land without trees

**llanura**
gran área de tierra llana sin árboles

© Discovery Education | www.discoveryeducation.com

**plateau**
a large, flat area of land that is higher than the other land around it

**meseta**
gran área de tierra llana que está a más altura que el terreno que la rodea

**pollen**
the yellow powder found inside a flower

**polen**
polvo amarillo que se encuentra dentro de una flor

**pollination**
moving or carrying pollen from a plant to make the seeds grow

**polinización**
transferencia o transporte de polen de una planta para hacer que crezcan las semillas

**preserve**
to protect or keep something safe

**preservar**
proteger o mantener algo a salvo

**property**
a characteristic of something

**propiedad**
característica de algo

—— Q ——

**quadrilateral**
a flat shape with four straight sides, such as a square or a parallelogram

**cuadrilátero**
figura plana con cuatro lados rectos, como un cuadrado o un paralelogramo

# R

**recycle**
to create new materials from something already used

**reciclar**
crear nuevos materiales a partir de algo usado

**relief map**
a type of map that shows how flat or steep the landforms are in an area

**mapa de relieve**
tipo de mapa que muestra si los accidentes geográficos son llanos o pronunciados en un área

**resource**
a material that can be used to solve problems

**recurso**
material que se puede usar para resolver problemas

**restore**
to put into use again

**restablecer**
volver a poner en servicio

**reverse engineering**
the process of learning about something by taking it apart to see how it works and what it is made of

**ingeniería inversa**
proceso de aprender acerca de algo, desarmándolo para ver cómo funciona y de qué está hecho

**river**

water flowing through a
landscape, usually fed by
smaller streams

**río**

agua que fluye a través de un
área, por lo general alimentada
por arroyos más pequeños

————— S —————

**select**

to choose or pick

**seleccionar**

elegir o escoger

**shelter**

a place that protects you from
harm or bad weather

**refugio**

lugar para protegerse de peligros
o el mal tiempo

**slope**

land that is slanted or angles
downward

**pendiente**

tierra inclinada hacia abajo

**soil**

dirt that covers Earth, in which
plants can grow and insects
can live

**suelo**

tierra que cubre nuestro planeta
en la que pueden crecer plantas y
vivir insectos

**solution**
a combination of two things that are mixed so well that each one cannot be picked out

**solución**
combinación de dos cosas que se mezclan tan bien que no se puede identificar cada una

**strategy**
a plan that can solve a problem

**estrategia**
plan que puede resolver un problema

**stream**
a small flowing body of water that starts with a spring and ends at a river

**arroyo**
pequeño cuerpo de agua que fluye y nace en una vertiente y termina en un río

**survive**
to continue to live

**sobrevivir**
continuar viviendo

——— T ———

**two-dimensional**
drawings and sketches that are done on flat paper to show width and height

**bidimensional**
dibujos y bosquejos que se hacen en papel plano para mostrar el ancho y la altura

## V

**valley**

the low place between two hills or mountains

**valle**

lugar bajo entre dos colinas o montañas

## W

**weathering**

the breakdown of rocks into smaller pieces called sediment

**meteorización**

desintegración de rocas en trozos más pequeños llamados sedimento

# Index

Discovery
EDUCATION